WHORING BRIDE

An Epistle to the Church in America

Whoring Bride

Elijah Washington

Published by Anchor Mountain Publishing, 2023.

WHORING BRIDE

First edition. June 7, 2023.

ISBN: 979-8223646020

Written by Elijah Washington.

ACKNOWLEDGMENTS

I want to thank my spiritual mentors in the faith, both past and present. Whether they know it or not, the growth in my spiritual formation is largely owing to their instruction. They have helped me to understand Scripture, offered loving rebukes, patient corrections, and grace upon grace whenever I fail. Their example is ever before me. They have been to me what Paul offered the Corinthians when he said, *"Be imitators of me, as I am of Christ."*

DEDICATION

I dedicate this book to my gracious Lord and Savior, Jesus Christ. He alone fully knew the depths of my unworthiness, yet loved me still. He willingly laid down His life so that I might be rescued from sin and death. More than that, He made it possible for me to be reconciled back to the Father and adopted into the family of God. While the filth and stench of sin covered me, He washed me clean of my unrighteousness. He has engraved His name upon my heart, and is preparing for me an eternal celebratory feast. For I was dead, and am alive again; I was lost, but now I'm found.

Preface

Let me be clear: I make no claim to have received divine inspiration while composing this letter. No one reading this work should conclude that these words carry the same weight or authority as sacred Scripture. Nor should this be viewed as an addendum to the Christian Bible. This author takes seriously the dangers of adding to or subtracting from *Holy Writ*.

Instead, I hope the following exhortations will function as a warning flare to professing Christians across the United States. To the degree we have navigated away from our divine mission, I pray the Holy Spirit will use this appeal as a course-correcting measure to help our churches return to faithful devotion. May we once again become doers of the word, and not hearers only.

Few people realize that some of the New Testament authors wrote pastoral letters to Christian congregations that were not included in the Bible. Though carrying apostolic authority, they weren't considered divinely inspired and were therefore never canonized as Scripture. This short book ought to be similarly categorized.

I have organized its sections with numerical chapters and verses for aesthetic purposes. There is no concern for sacrilege on this point because the chapter and verse notations in our Bibles were not in the original manuscripts. They were added for convenience many generations after the books were written.

In his letter to the church in Rome, Saint Paul wrote about the affection he had for his Jewish kinsmen. More than once he described how his heart was burdened for his countrymen. This sentiment resonates with me. You should know that I consider myself a patriot. I love my country and I love my fellow

Americans. However, as Christ-followers, our citizenship in Heaven supersedes our citizenship on Earth. We are constrained to pledge our highest allegiance to Christ Jesus and His eternal kingdom. Loyalty to Him trumps national patriotism. Where the deeds and virtues of America align with the kingdom of God, we can rejoice as proud Americans. But when the values of our homeland are diametrically opposed to the King of Kings, the primacy of our devotion rightly belongs to Him, not America. (We'll explore this further in chapter five.)

A word about the title. My phrasing is meant to invoke a shocking and unsettling image. Adultery is a crushing betrayal. Marital unfaithfulness is bad enough, but the idea of "whoring" suggests selling one's affections to multiple lovers. In the Bible, God enters into a covenantal relationship with His redeemed people similar to that of a marriage. The language of spiritual infidelity was sometimes used as a metaphor to describe the betrayal God feels when His people turn their backs on Him. Giving our worship to rival lovers is spiritual adultery. I believe the provocative descriptor of a "whoring bride" accurately portrays our spiritual unfaithfulness today.

A word about the author. I am writing under a pseudonym. My age, gender, race, marital status, and socio-economic background are of little importance. In a time where words are evaluated by the speaker's location within a hierarchy of privilege/oppression, I am writing anonymously in the hopes that this book will stand or fall on its own merit. The worthiness or unworthiness of the messenger should not detract from the validity of the message. Let these words be accepted or rejected based solely on their truthfulness according to Scripture. Some might accuse me of cowardice for not disclosing my true identity.

WHORING BRIDE

I respect that opinion but am content to let God judge the reasons for my anonymity.

If this publication is broadly accepted, I am not seeking personal recognition for its success. My sole aim is to serve the Church in America by sounding an alarm, highlighting the worldly influences corrupting her worship.

Oftentimes when Jesus taught, He added the caveat *"He who has ears to hear, let him hear."* He once told a parable of a farmer who purchased seed and began generously sowing the seed on all types of terrain, most of which yielded no fruit. Jesus told this story to illustrate how spreading the message of the kingdom works in conjunction with the human heart.

I hope that what I have written will land on fertile soil within the hearts of many readers. However, I am fully expecting some to reject it outright, for not all sinners positively respond to a call for repentance. I only ask my readers to keep an open mind when considering these exhortations. Insofar as these words ring true, I pray that the Holy Spirit will do what I cannot—convict us of the pervasive sin in our midst, and lead us to repentance.

If I have written anything amiss, let those words be ignored and forgotten, forever cast into the ash heap of history. Before proceeding, I ask that you first pray the words of the Psalmist, and allow the Holy Spirit to dictate how you should feel regarding this work. *"Search me, O God, and know my heart! Try me and know my thoughts! And see if there be any grievous way in me, and lead me in the way everlasting!"*

Soli Deo Gloria,
Elijah Washington

ELIJAH WASHINGTON

* The English Standard Version (ESV) translation of the Bible is used for all scriptural passages quoted in the following chapters. Consistent with the tone and style of New Testament epistles, the specific reference details for quoted passages are not included in the body of the text.

WHORING BRIDE

"Hear the word of the Lord, O children of Israel, for the Lord has a controversy with the inhabitants of the land. There is no faithfulness or steadfast love...For a spirit of whoredom has led them astray, and they have left their God to play the whore." Hosea 4:1, 12

Chapter 1: Redeemed

1 To the collective churches in the United States, ransomed by God for His eternal purpose. Spanning from coast to coast in diverse expressions of worship and theological distinctives, I send you my greetings in the name of our Lord and Savior Jesus Christ. 2 Like most of you, I am one who was nurtured into faith by the grace of God in the land of the free and home of the brave.

3 My journeys throughout our country have allowed me to visit many of your congregations. Your skilled teachers and gifted musicians are impressive, drawing many who are spiritually hungry to your worship gatherings. 4 God in His mercy has preserved a faithful remnant holding fast to the hope of the gospel, safeguarding the spiritual inheritance we received from those who came before us. However, sin has increasingly taken root within our fellowships.

5 With great patience, God has long suffered the shame of our spiritual unfaithfulness. As the Apostle Paul mentioned in his letter to the Corinthians, God will not be mocked indefinitely. 6 The Church in America must renounce her unfaithfulness or risk being cut off from His divine blessing and protection. Many of you are in danger of falling away from the faith entirely, led astray by the sins of our culture.

7 Over time we allowed a subtle and creeping darkness to take residence in our midst. For too long we have tolerated the destructive allurements of sin, contaminating our worship of the one true God. 8 To my utter shame, I too am guilty of spiritual unfaithfulness. I write this letter in hopes that you will join me in casting off the entanglements of sin, recovering our place as obedient sons and daughters of light in America. 9 Through

repentance, I pray we carry the torch of our faith without faltering in this late hour. A steadfast and sincere witness is needed in our country now more than ever.

10 It is abundantly clear that we have forgotten our true identity. The gifts of liberty and prosperity have caused many of us to grow lazy and forsake the high calling we have in Christ as ambassadors of His kingdom. 11 We have divided our loyalties between our Redeemer and the enticing promises of sin. 12 Believing ourselves to be wise, we have become fools thinking that we can retain the Lord's favor while courting love affairs with the vices of Satan. 13 Our God revealed himself to Moses as a consuming fire; a jealous God who will not share his covenant bride with another.

14 Adam and Eve were tempted by the cunning serpent and believed his words over the promises of the Creator. Their choice to disobey God disrupted the perfect order of His creation. 15 He could not maintain His holiness and justice by sweeping the sins of mankind under the rug. Therefore God cursed the ground He created, allowing Adam and Eve to feel the sting of sin through pain and mortal death. 16 It infected all of creation, introducing an ongoing plague of broken fellowship between us and our Maker. None are exempt.

17 All of us, from generation to generation, are born into this world with a proclivity to prefer darkness rather than light. We participate in this cosmic rebellion when our innate desires—the fallenness of our flesh—choose sin over obedience to God.

18 The consequences of sin are manifold, chiefly that it earns us eternal condemnation. 19 There is no amount of effort or

moral action we could accomplish to save ourselves. We all have trespassed the law of God, falling short of His perfect standards.

20 However, God being slow to anger and rich in mercy chose to postpone the verdict of man's total condemnation. 21 In His eternal wisdom, so that in the coming ages He might display the bounty of His grace, He planned to absorb the full punishment of our sins into Himself, thus creating a way for mankind to be saved. 22 God desired that none should perish, but all to receive the free gift of salvation. Thus began His great story of redemption.

23 The nature of God's divine personhood is a mystery, but He revealed Himself to the world as a perfect harmony of three persons, eternally unified: Father, Son, and Holy Spirit. 24 In His foreknowledge, God chose the descendants of Jacob as the lineage through which His savior would be revealed to mankind. The offer of redemption appeared first to the house of Israel and was then opened up to all the nations of the world.

25 Jesus Christ, the only begotten Son of the Father, entered our world, being born in the likeness of man, yet without sin. 26 In this way God lived among us, subjecting Himself to the fragile and sorrow-ridden limitations of mankind as the promised deliverer who would bear the eternal punishment for our sins.

27 Christ Jesus, being the spotless Lamb of God, offered His life as a ransom sacrifice to die in our stead. He volunteered to take all our shame and guilt upon His shoulders if we would but repent of our sins and believe in His name. 28 To those who place their trust in Him, Jesus promised to repair the broken fellowship with our Creator and welcome us back into His family as sons and daughters of the Most High.

29 But even the curse of death could not ultimately defeat Jesus. On the third day following His execution, Christ triumphed over the grave and rose again. 30 The perfect obedience that Jesus achieved would be transferred to us sinners by grace through faith in Him.

31 After rising from the dead, Christ appeared to His followers and gave them instructions on how His kingdom would unfold in the world, thereby undoing the curse of sin. He then ascended back to His Father's side to reign forevermore as Lord of the universe. 32 The good news of His life, death, resurrection, ascension, and imminent return to make all things new is the gospel we received and proclaim to the world.

33 Christ purposed to establish His reign on Earth just as it is in Heaven, reversing the damage done to His creation through sin. The teachings of Jesus recorded in Scripture lay out the ethics of His kingdom. 34 In the kingdom of God, the last are first and the first are last. In the kingdom of God, it is the poor who are rich and the rich who are poor. In His kingdom, you don't hate your enemies but love them. 35 We are not to return evil when evil has been done to us. Instead, we are to do good and pray for those who wish us harm. 36 Love is the highest virtue in the kingdom of God. As ones who have been forgiven of much, we are to freely forgive others when they wrong us.

37 God has revealed to us His plan of remaking the world, unifying Heaven and Earth. We who have tasted the delights of this glorious redemption have been commissioned as the agents by which His salvation will reach the ends of the world. 38 Our calling is not merely to secure for ourselves a safe and happy afterlife, but also to join God in His renewal project. 39 We

participate in the world's redemption through radical demonstrations of love and sacrifice.

40 This will come about when the ransomed sons and daughters of God follow in the footsteps of their martyred Savior, emulating His example. 41 One sure thing Jesus promised is that we would face persecution and all kinds of dangers as we obey His commands. 42 The world misunderstood him, so the world will misunderstand us. They maligned and mistreated Him, and we should expect no better treatment. 43 Jesus said, *"A disciple is not above his teacher, but everyone when he is fully trained will be like his teacher."* In other words, if they hated Him, they will likewise hate us.

44 To our shame, this is not how we are viewed by our culture. The world mocks us because our hypocrisy is evident to all. 45 They do not reject us because our lives reflect that of Christ Jesus. Instead, they sneer and disregard our message because our actions demonstrate that we are ensnared by all the entanglements we were meant to oppose.

46 Our churches have become gatherings of sanctified worldliness. We have dethroned God as the primary object of worship and replaced Him with carnal gratification. 47 We claim a spiritual marriage with our Creator while groping the voluptuous temptations of sinful indulgence. 48 Our witness to a weary world was supposed to be that of lives radically transformed by redeeming grace. Instead, we have become like a whoring, unfaithful bride. 49 How can we say that we truly love God and follow Jesus while worshiping the idols of our culture?

Chapter 2: Idolatry

1 Early in the story of redemption, our God revealed Himself as *"One."* He appeared to Moses in the burning bush and instructed him to go to the children of Israel enslaved by Pharaoh and inform them that their deliverance was soon forthcoming. 2 Moses said, *"If I come to the people of Israel and say to them, 'The God of your fathers has sent me to you,' and they ask me, 'What is his name?' what shall I say to them?"* 3 The reply Moses received would shape Israel's identity for generations to come. God said to Moses, *"'I AM WHO I AM.' And he said, 'Say this to the people of Israel: 'I AM has sent me to you.'"*

4 Until that day, God had not revealed His name to mankind. Referring to Himself as "I AM" was to be foundational in our understanding of His nature. 5 Later, when giving instructions on how they should operate as God's chosen people, He said, *"Hear, O Israel: The LORD our God, the LORD is one. You shall love the LORD your God with all your heart and with all your soul and with all your might. And these words that I command you today shall be on your heart. You shall teach them diligently to your children, and shall talk of them when you sit in your house, and when you walk by the way, and when you lie down, and when you rise. You shall bind them as a sign on your hand, and they shall be as frontlets between your eyes. You shall write them on the doorposts of your house and on your gates."*

6 When Moses ascended Mount Sinai to receive God's law, the first two instructions were, *"You shall have no other gods before me. You shall not make for yourself an image in the form of anything in heaven above or on the earth beneath or in the waters below. You shall not bow down to them or worship them; for I, the*

Lord your God, am a jealous God, punishing the children for the sin of the parents to the third and fourth generation of those who hate me, but showing love to a thousand generations of those who love me and keep my commandments." 7 God was adamant about preserving the loyal worship of His people. He was not willing to share His glory with another.

8 It is a mistake to think of idols merely as statues within pagan cultures. Anything can become an idol—visible or invisible, wholesome or immoral. 9 Idolatry is the grievous sin of looking to something else besides God for what He alone should be. Treasuring lesser things as an ultimate thing dethrones God from His rightful place in our hearts and minds. 10 Whatever we serve above God becomes our new master. That which we devote our lives to above God becomes an idol. Whoever we love more than God becomes our spiritual mistress.

11 There is indeed only one God, and He has no equal. In that sense, there are no other gods besides the great I AM. He claimed as much speaking to the prophet Jeremiah when He said, *"Can man make for himself gods? Such are not gods!"* 12 With these words God showed that idols are not competing deities. He has no rivals in that regard. Yet, we rob God of the glory He deserves by seeking fulfillment in other places when He alone is all we need.

13 Long ago, worship of God for the children of Israel was contained within a tabernacle and eventually a temple, facilitated by a strict priestly order of sacrifices and offerings. But when Jesus arrived, He opened up access for all people to worship God.

WHORING BRIDE

14 When speaking with a Samaritan woman inquiring about certain holy mountains and temples Jesus said to her, *"But the hour is coming, and is now here, when the true worshipers will worship the Father in spirit and truth, for the Father is seeking such people to worship him. God is spirit, and those who worship him must worship in spirit and truth."* 15 Saying this, Jesus was claiming that true worship isn't about sacred locations, but a matter of the heart. Christ clearly illustrated that God is still passionate about us worshiping Him. 16 We were created to worship our Maker and nothing short of that can truly satisfy the longings of our hearts. We err when we seek soul fulfillment elsewhere.

17 Not only does the misdirected worship of idols leave us unsatisfied, but it is also a great insult to God. Such worship is no less an offense to God in our day than it was under the old covenant. Jesus negating the need for temples and priestly sacrifices does not mean that God is now apathetic about our worship.

18 Christ has knocked down all impediments that stand in the way of us giving our unrivaled worship to the Father. His sacrifice made us worthy to enter God's presence. 19 The veil covering the holy of holies was torn in two, clearing a path for us to approach Him with an acceptable righteousness, having washed away the stain of our guilt. Through Christ, we can live in perpetual communion with God in prayerful devotion.

20 What then prevents us from worshiping God as He desires? It is our love affair with the enticing pleasure of this world. 21 We would rather frolic around in the sewage of our God-hating culture than drink from the fountain of living water.

Have you forgotten that we were called to live a life set apart from those who reject our God? 22 We all want our sins forgiven but many are not also willing to leave our adulterous lovers. We falsely believe they are more satisfying than God.

23 Diligence in your vocations is not a sin. But if success in your career is more important to you than building and advancing His kingdom, you're serving an idol. 24 If finding a spouse or the well-being of your family is more valuable to you than your calling as adopted sons and daughters in the family of God, you've twisted that blessing into an idol. 25 If appetites of the flesh—food, sex, safety, comfort--are a higher priority than personal sacrifice for the sake of others, you have an idol. 26 If earning and keeping a lot of money for personal security is more important to you than radical generosity, you are clinging to an idol. 27 If being admired by the world never yields to the prospect of being slandered or thought foolish because of your costly obedience to Jesus, this is your idol.

28 My dear brothers and sisters, the abundance of blessings we enjoy in America presents a dangerous threat to our worship of God. We glut ourselves on the comforts at our disposal and have grown addicted to the pleasures of this world. 29 Remember that our days are numbered and we are not promised a tomorrow. In light of eternity, our time on Earth is like a vapor. 30 Very soon we shall breathe our last breath and stand before God to give an account of our lives. 31 Anticipate the regret you will feel at that moment for courting so many idols while on Earth. Consider that day and work now to rearrange your priorities before it's too late.

32 The glorious truth for those saved and redeemed by Jesus is that no condemnation remains on us. We will not have to pay for our sins because Jesus already settled that debt on our behalf. 33 On Judgment Day believers in Christ will receive rewards according to their faithfulness and obedience to Him. But hoping to be saved in the end without renouncing our carnal habits is no safe bet for the believer.

34 Recall the words of our Lord who said, *"Either make the tree good and its fruit good, or make the tree bad and its fruit bad, for the tree is known by its fruit."* 35 The final judgment will reveal if our lives were made new by grace, yielding a harvest of good fruit, or reveal that we remained in our worldliness, unchanged by grace and therefore yielding nothing but bad fruit.

36 Do not be mistaken. If the message of forgiveness sounds appealing, but we're not willing to be transformed into the likeness of Christ through obedience to His commands, we must ask ourselves whether or not the gospel has penetrated our hearts. 37 The Apostle Paul addressed similar concerns with the Corinthian church and instructed them to *"test"* themselves and examine to see if they were truly in the faith. We do well to heed that warning today.

38 The Prophet Hosea issued similar warnings in his day to the people of Israel. The tribe of Ephraim had abandoned faithful devotion to God, turning instead to serve the idols of their culture. God spoke through Hosea to the tribe of Judah and warned them not to emulate the choices of Ephraim. 39 He said, *"Ephraim is joined with idols; leave him alone."* This is a terrifying prophetic word because it implied that God had already made up His mind about them. As if a divine judgment was imminent.

40 Likewise in our day, it reveals an error in our thinking if we believe that God will not similarly judge the churches in America for their idolatry. 41 The judgment of God is not always active with fire and brimstone. Sometimes it can be the passive removal of His blessing and protection, allowing us to endure the due consequences of our misplaced worship. 42 If we will not confess our sins and forsake our idols, do not be deceived into thinking that God will be pleased with our religious activity.

43 To say we belong to Christ while fondling idols is a farce. Persisting in spiritual unfaithfulness tramples God's love and plays Him for a fool. We become like the whoring bride who continues with her multitude of lovers.

Chapter 3: Sexuality

1 Sexual intercourse was not the accidental discovery of mankind's instinctual curiosity. It is God who conceived the idea and masterfully designed our bodies to enjoy the act. 2 He blessed and sanctioned sex within the confines of heterosexual marriage for two reasons: the pleasure of intimacy with one's spouse, and the procreation of children. 3 There is a proper way to enjoy the gift of sex as it was intended, but like most gifts from above, the fallenness of man has twisted and corrupted it beyond comprehension.

4 It is no surprise when those far from God indulge their basest sexual impulses. They are blind to spiritual truth and know not what they do. 5 The children of light, however, are not to view sex as the world does. We must only partake within the boundaries set forth by our Maker. 6 Out of reverence for God we are to follow the clear instructions of Scripture, thus honoring His perfect design. I wish that I could commend you on this point, but we have allowed the values of our culture to shape our view and practice of human sexuality.

7 The desire for sex is a natural appetite of the body. Our souls long for intimacy and the body craves the physical fulfillment of that desire. 8 Likewise, food is also a natural appetite requiring physical satiation. As is the case with all such physical appetites, there are carnal ways of gratifying them which seem harmless, but work against the purpose for which the gift was given.

9 Eating too much food or the wrong kinds of food will damage our bodies, leading to disease and personal misery. So it is with sexual intercourse. 10 Indulging in the act outside of the

parameters established by Scripture not only dishonors God but invites needless shame and anguish into the lives of those who misuse the gift. Doing so thus leads to all kinds of emotional and societal wreckage.

11 Those who walk in darkness laugh and scorn at our sexual ethics. They cannot comprehend denying themselves full, unrestricted gratification because they are enslaved to their cravings. 12 Their god is in their loins and compels them to sacrifice their sexual purity at the altar of their corrupted desires. It ought not to be so with you, for we know our Maker and the purposes for which He created us.

13 And now brothers and sisters, I must address what many of you lack the courage to teach in your gatherings. 14 It is understandable why you shy away from this difficult truth because it is so hated by our culture. Nothing will incite wrathful contempt like challenging their sexual practices. But here we are constrained by sacred Scripture. 15 We must fear God more than the indignation of American culture. 16 It is a sin for any man to have sex with a woman who is not his wife. Likewise, it is a sin for any woman to have sex with a man who is not her husband. 17 Moreover, it is a sin for a man to have sex with another man, and it is a sin for a woman to have sex with another woman. 18 It is a sin for an adult to have sex with a child. These acts are indulged and celebrated in our country every day, but they are detestable to God.

19 Sharing these truths will be difficult because our society will violently resist hearing them. There are some in our midst today who have crafted and spread sophisticated arguments for why these ancient beliefs need not apply to us today. 20 They

have been deceived into thinking God's chief end for our happiness is the fulfillment of our sexual yearnings, whatever those may be. 21 Do not listen to such ones. Some of them are false teachers influenced by demonic powers. Others are merely displaying their naivety and ignorance. 22 They have compromised their conscience to justify their cravings. Rather than embracing self-denial and the transforming power of God which raised Christ from the dead, they cave to their lustful passions.

23 There are some among you with sincere motives. Christ showed compassion to sinners and you seek to do likewise. 24 God is no doubt honored by your concern for those outside the faith. But you do them no favors by celebrating and enabling their sin. Keep in mind the example of our Lord, who offered forgiveness and friendship to all who would believe in Him, but never endorsed their sinful behavior. 25 Christ showed sincere love toward the lost soul while unambiguously declaring *"Go and sin no more."*

26 Out of fear, we have softened our language regarding the virtues of biblical sexuality. In the name of tolerance, we have endorsed deviant behavior. 27 Because of our lack of courage and righteous fortitude, the ravages of sexual sin have destroyed countless lives within our congregations. 28 Our men have disgraced themselves and their God through shameful exploits. Our women have debased themselves searching for affirmation which leaves them feeling used and empty. 29 We have poisoned our minds with the proliferation of indecent images. 30 We are slaves to our immoral lust, yet rather than being set free we prefer to caress our chains. 31 There are even some in our churches who

use their mantle of leadership to sexually prey on the vulnerable. 32 I can think of no greater shame than to use spiritual authority as a means to gratify one's depraved lusts. 33 Other leaders turn a blind eye to allegations of abuse and molestation, covering over sin instead of exposing them. Such leaders ought to be driven out of our churches. 34 Wolves should not be entrusted with caring for little lambs.

35 Beyond the pervasive sexual sins we tolerate within our congregations, I'm now hearing that some of you are embracing the view that gender is not a fixed reality. 36 Brothers and sisters, do not be deceived. Each of us was carefully knit together by God in the wombs of our mothers. 37 All the days of our lives are planned and orchestrated in the Father's mind before one of them comes to pass. He knows the number of hairs on our heads. 38 Despite our flaws, God loves each one of us just as we are, and He makes no mistakes. 39 The idea that some are born in the wrong body is a pernicious lie from the Evil One. Lying is his native tongue and he aims only to steal, kill, and destroy God's beloved. 40 Let the discerning reader understand: the spirit of Moloch endures and holds sway in our culture. Do not sacrifice your children on his altar.

41 Have you become so comfortable with debauchery in our worship gatherings that you are willing to blur the lines of how God created male and female genders in His image? 42 Are you so eager to win the approval of a wicked and adulterous generation that you'll celebrate sexual perversion and the mutilation of young children? God forbid! 43 Surely Paul's warning to Timothy is relevant for us: "*I charge you in the presence of God and of Christ Jesus, who is to judge the living and*

the dead, and by his appearing and his kingdom: preach the word; be ready in season and out of season; reprove, rebuke, and exhort, with complete patience and teaching. For the time is coming when people will not endure sound teaching, but having itching ears they will accumulate for themselves teachers to suit their own passions, and will turn away from listening to the truth and wander off into myths. As for you, always be sober-minded, endure suffering, do the work of an evangelist, fulfill your ministry."

44 Brothers and sisters, I fear that many of our churches have become monuments endorsing wickedness rather than outposts for saving sinners. 45 Recall to mind the recent teachings you've heard. Do they challenge and confront the carnal values of our culture or validate them with ear-tickling approval?

46 Again, I am speaking of those within the body of Christ. The Apostle Paul instructed the church in Corinth *"I wrote to you in my letter not to associate with sexually immoral people—not at all meaning the sexually immoral of this world, or the greedy and swindlers, or idolaters, since then you would need to go out of the world. But now I am writing to you not to associate with anyone who bears the name of brother if he is guilty of sexual immorality or greed, or is an idolater, reviler, drunkard, or swindler—not even to eat with such a one. For what have I to do with judging outsiders? Is it not those inside the church whom you are to judge? God judges those outside. 'Purge the evil person from among you.'"*

47 What convinced you that we can disregard this stern warning in our churches today? Has God changed His mind? Must God now update His moral prescriptions to accommodate our cultural preferences? 48 Following this logic (I'm speaking now as a fool), perhaps we should force God to modernize His archaic views on adultery, bestiality, theft, lying, and murder!

49 Who are you, O man, to question the Eternal One? Your counterfeit wisdom is a sham. 50 Presuming to lecture God will only solidify your delusion.

51 Those who are spiritually blind, enslaved to their sexual cravings, or confused about their identities should more rightly be the objects of our compassion rather than disdain. The same carnal lust which presently rules their bodies is the same master which previously ruled ours. We were dead in our sins and helpless to save ourselves. 52 But thanks be to God, we have been delivered from our former way of life. Jesus has redeemed us from destruction and washed us clean in His blood. More than that, the Holy Spirit was deposited into our hearts to sanctify us into a holy people.

53 I am happy to report that there is no sexual sin so grievous that God cannot forgive. He loves the homosexual sinner as much as the heterosexual sinner and willingly died for both. So why is it that some of you will shame the former while tolerating the latter?

54 Sexual sin does not disqualify you from the mercy and grace of God offered to us in Christ. All of us are guilty of sexual sin, whether in the body or the mind. 55 The shame of your past or the present cravings in your body might lead some of you to conclude that sexual purity is hopeless. Banish the thought! 56 Christ can forgive the worst offenders because the merit of His sacrifice exceeds the defilement of your sins. 57 The lyric of the Psalmist rings true: *"For as high as the heavens are above the earth, so great is his steadfast love toward those who fear him; as far as the east is from the west, so far does he remove our transgressions from us."*

WHORING BRIDE

58 Forgiveness of sexual sin is available for those who embrace Christ by faith, but more than that, liberation from destructive habits and corrupting desires is also possible by the sanctifying work of the Holy Spirit within us. 59 Hence, Paul exhorted the Corinthians saying, *"Flee from sexual immorality. Every other sin a person commits is outside the body, but the sexually immoral person sins against his own body. Or do you not know that your body is a temple of the Holy Spirit within you, whom you have from God? You are not your own, for you were bought with a price. So glorify God in your body."* 60 We must adamantly reject all forms of sexual sin while offering the mercy and grace of the gospel to any repentant sinner.

61 Though we continue to wrestle against the flesh, we have hope that we will one day be made whole. At Christ's return, our remaining corruption will be eradicated once and for all, and we will dwell with God in eternal righteousness. 62 Until that day, we must continually reckon ourselves dead to sin as we pray for the grace to walk in obedience.

63 Therefore, I urge you to rely fully on the power of the Holy Spirit to resist the temptations of lustful indulgence. 64 What Saint Paul wrote to the church in Rome is true for us as well: *"For if you live according to the flesh you will die, but if by the Spirit you put to death the deeds of the body, you will live."* 65 So step out of the sludge of sexual sin and be cleansed. Consecrate yourself to God as a pure and wholesome bride, faithful to her spiritual Husband.

Chapter 4: Money

1 A common misconception is that money itself is evil. This cannot be true for God is wealthier than all the combined riches of mankind. 2 He owns every inch of land on this good earth, as well as all the inhabitants therein. Every mountain, every valley, every stream, every building, every last coin and purse, and all living creatures are rightfully His. 3 God dispenses wealth to us as He pleases.

4 Our country has enjoyed prosperity unlike that of most nations throughout history. This is not the first time God has entrusted people with inordinate wealth. 5 Our fathers Abraham, Isaac, Jacob, and David (among others) were granted earthly riches. 6 This was not sinful gain on their part but divine providence for an expressed purpose: they were blessed to be a blessing to others. 7 America was granted financial abundance to likewise be a blessing to the needy of the world.

8 Some among you have leveraged their wealth to serve the needs of their community and those around the world. Such ones are to be commended for their generosity. 9 They have pleased their Father in Heaven by doing so, for the wisdom of Solomon says, *"Whoever is generous to the poor lends to the Lord, and he will repay him for his deed."* 10 But I need to remind you of a parable our Lord shared with His disciples regarding the hour in which the Son of Man would return. 11 He told the story of a master going away to a wedding feast. Some servants were faithfully doing their work and when the master returned, he rewarded them for their obedience. 12 But some servants thought to themselves "My master is delayed in returning" and wastefully indulged in lavish feasting and drinking. When the

master returned and saw the unfaithful servants, they were severely punished. 13 Driving the point home, Jesus ended the parable by saying, *"Everyone to whom much was given, of him much will be required."*

14 Brothers and sisters, you are not owners of the resources you receive, but stewards of your Master's wealth. In the end, each of us will give an account of what we did with the money entrusted to us. 15 Do not make the mistake of judging your stewardship against those much wealthier than you. Some are given more and some are given less, but all of it belongs to God. 16 He expects us to leverage what we have for His eternal purposes.

17 It is not wrong to earn money. Nor is it evil to accumulate money. 18 Some of you have been uniquely gifted to multiply wealth through skills of industry. These are important colaborers of the gospel, for they are used by God to fund kingdom advancement.

19 However, in some of our churches we seem to have forgotten the warnings of Scripture regarding wealth. Jesus said, *"Truly, I say to you, only with difficulty will a rich person enter the kingdom of heaven. Again I tell you, it is easier for a camel to go through the eye of a needle than for a rich person to enter the kingdom of God."* 20 We might mistakenly think this does not apply to us because we do not view ourselves as rich, but this is not true. 21 By comparison, the average earner in our congregations is exponentially more wealthy than our brothers and sisters around the world. The opulence of our modern conveniences has clouded our judgment. 22 Most nations are not afforded the same economic freedoms and opportunities

that we've enjoyed, so we ought to be mindful of our privileged estate. 23 The abundance of wealth that we have been given should be viewed as an opportunity to generously invest in the kingdom of God.

24 So what explanation can be offered to justify our stinginess and greed? Is it not that we have been lured away from trusting God as our provider? 25 We have been enticed by the luxuries of this world and dedicated ourselves to markers of status and worldly comforts. Many of us have become lovers of money rather than lovers of God. 26 Saint Paul's advice to young Timothy ought to instruct our current position: *"But godliness with contentment is great gain, for we brought nothing into the world, and we cannot take anything out of the world. But if we have food and clothing, with these we will be content. But those who desire to be rich fall into temptation, into a snare, into many senseless and harmful desires that plunge people into ruin and destruction. For the love of money is a root of all kinds of evils. It is through this craving that some have wandered away from the faith and pierced themselves with many pangs."*

27 Having money is not evil, but the lure of what it promises is fatal. 28 The Devil tempted Eve in the garden with the fruit saying, *"For God knows that when you eat of it your eyes will be opened, and you will be like God, knowing good and evil."* 29 Eve believed the serpent because she wanted to be like God.

30 Brothers and sisters, we are presently beguiled by the same lie. We are being plunged into ruinous destruction because we have fallen in love with the Master's bountiful wealth over the Master Himself. 31 Falsely, we believe that we too can be like God, providing for ourselves instead of trusting in Him. The love

of money and the eagerness to become wealthy has deceived us into prioritizing our own desires over relying on God to meet our needs as we invest in the kingdom. 32 Are we exempt in America from having to trust God for our daily needs? We demonstrate small faith when we rely on our own resourcefulness in place of utter dependence on God. Has His power diminished through the ages? Is He no longer capable of doing miracles in our day? 33 We forfeit divine providence and supernatural blessing by trusting in ourselves over the God who holds all things together by the word of His power.

34 So what then? Are we all commanded to live as paupers? Not so. Wise stewardship is a godly trait. We honor God by taking seriously the responsibilities we have to our families. 35 The divine wisdom of Solomon states: *A good man leaves an inheritance to his children's children.* And the Apostle Paul wrote, *"But if anyone does not provide for his relatives, and especially for members of his household, he has denied the faith and is worse than an unbeliever."* 36 There is no standard of living universally prescribed to us by Scripture. Rather, we are to view the money we have as an opportunity to honor God with the resources He entrusted to us. 37 Handle your affairs, but resist the temptation for extravagant living. 38 Earn and save and invest and give in such a way that any bookkeeper can see you value the kingdom of God more than your own comforts. 39 Radical generosity ought to be the prevailing posture within our gatherings.

40 To those barely scraping by, perhaps you are experiencing financial hardships because of your own bad decisions. There is grace for you. 41 Confess your sins and believe that God can

redeem you from the pit you have dug for yourselves. Cry out to God in the hour of your need and trust Him for deliverance. 42 God is rich in mercy and can undo any disaster that you have created. Others of you have never enjoyed lavish wealth because of your low estate. 43 To you, I offer the comforting words of our Lord Jesus who said, "*Therefore I tell you, do not be anxious about your life, what you will eat or what you will drink, nor about your body, what you will put on. Is not life more than food, and the body more than clothing? Look at the birds of the air: they neither sow nor reap nor gather into barns, and yet your heavenly Father feeds them. Are you not of more value than they? And which of you by being anxious can add a single hour to his span of life? And why are you anxious about clothing? Consider the lilies of the field, how they grow: they neither toil nor spin, yet I tell you, even Solomon in all his glory was not arrayed like one of these. But if God so clothes the grass of the field, which today is alive and tomorrow is thrown into the oven, will he not much more clothe you, O you of little faith? Therefore do not be anxious, saying, 'What shall we eat?' or 'What shall we drink?' or 'What shall we wear?' For the Gentiles seek after all these things, and your heavenly Father knows that you need them all. But seek first the kingdom of God and his righteousness, and all these things will be added to you.*"

44 Needlessly worrying about your financial situation cannot solve your problems, and shows a lack of faith. Your Father in Heaven is exuberantly wealthy and knows exactly what you need. 45 More than that, He has promised to take care of all your needs if you'll but trust Him as you seek first and foremost the kingdom of God. You may not be able to give as others can, but unworried faith and generosity should still be an indelible mark on your life.

46 Lastly, on this subject, I must address those elevated as pastors and leaders within your churches. Are you not to lead by example? 47 You are not exempt from these expectations simply because of the office you hold. How can your people be expected to sacrifice their comforts in the pursuit of generosity when you are not? 48 Yes, a worker is worth his wages, and those who devote their lives to gospel ministry can justly draw their livelihood from the gospel, but some of you use this as an excuse to enrich yourselves. 49 You prey on naive believers, misleading them to give sacrificially while spending those resources on yourselves. 50 Promising riches to those who give, you mismanage their tithes and offerings by adding house to house, luxury upon luxury in your secret worship of mammon. You should be ashamed of yourselves! 51 Surely the rebuke of Jesus applies to you when He said, *"No one can serve two masters, for either he will hate the one and love the other, or he will be devoted to the one and despise the other. You cannot serve God and money."* 52 Serving the body of Christ is a high and holy calling, not an opportunity for selfish gain.

53 So I urge you, brothers and sisters, to risk much in your service to God. Our Father in Heaven knows our needs and has promised to meet them according to His riches in glory. 54 We can therefore restructure our priorities with strategic and radical generosity as we appropriately steward His resources for the sake of the gospel.

Chapter 5: Politics

1 Churches in America, it grieves me to point out that most of us have fallen into a trap. 2 Despite our strength in numbers, long ago we lost our prophetic voice. We unwittingly corralled ourselves into opposing camps arguing over temporal matters. 3 We were suckered into elevating our views of national policy over the primacy of the gospel, treating each other as reviled enemies rather than spiritual siblings and co-laborers in the kingdom of God. This ought not to be so among the redeemed sons and daughters of the Most High.

4 Here we may be tempted to justify our behavior. Each of us drawn into the contentious debates of today are convinced that we are serving God by fighting for our political preferences. 5 But if our affiliations lead us to despise those on the other side then we must be honest and admit that we have been co-opted by the power brokers in our world, thus compromising our mission.

6 It is true, our faith is political in nature and is meant to guide our involvement in society. Faithfully serving God means loving the world as He does, seeking the good of our neighbors regardless if they believe like us or not. 7 We should grapple with the issues of our day because we are called to regard the tangible needs of others. However, resolving those issues is not easily achieved. 8 Instead of standing united for the good of our neighbors, we have broken fellowship with each other and divided ourselves into the political factions of our culture.

9 Both sides agree that education is a moral good, but have different opinions on how educational systems ought to be organized. 10 Both sides care about the poor but offer varying solutions to their plight. 11 We all recognize that maintaining

a clean, healthy infrastructure is desirable but Scripture gives us no directives on roads or waste management. 12 All citizens, believing and unbelieving, want safe communities but cannot agree on the best manner to address crime. 13 Who can help solve these problems if not the people of God? 14 What is a king or prime minister or president, if not a fallible human? What are lawmakers? Are they not men and women of the earth with corruptible desires like our own? 15 But where leaders of this world fall short, we are capable of helping mankind because we draw from supernatural resources. 16 We have the wherewithal to offer meaningful solutions to the ills that plague our communities but have chosen instead to enter the trenches of mudslinging with the warring parties.

17 At the heart of our faith is a man dying for his enemies, praying for those who mistreat him. 18 Though we tend to ignore this teaching, Jesus himself said, *"If you love those who love you, what benefit is that to you? For even sinners love those who love them. And if you do good to those who do good to you, what benefit is that to you? For even sinners do the same."* 19 Does this describe your political philosophy? The values of the kingdom are to inform and direct our civic engagement, but political victories must not come at the expense of alienating our neighbors—much less each other. 20 Our allegiance to Christ must supersede any agreements we share with the policy positions of our preferred candidates.

21 The Lord came not just to save sinners from eternal damnation but also to establish His kingdom reign on Earth as it is in Heaven. 22 He aims once and for all to reverse the curse of sin. Jesus promised to return one day and complete His work of

redemption with the total restoration of all things. 23 In the end, Christ will reclaim everything He has made and bring it under His sovereign rule as Lord of the universe.

24 When the early followers of Christ declared "Jesus is Lord" they were simultaneously acknowledging that Caesar was not. To claim "Jesus is Lord and the United States government is not" is no less scandalous. 25 Regrettably, this does not describe the political climate within our churches. We have aligned ourselves with politicians and party affiliations rather than working together on a united front.

26 What has obstructed your vision from seeing what is plainly true? Are you so fearful of criticism that you will ignore the destruction of the innocent? 27 Some of you are quick to say "love is love" and "hate is hate" but refuse to admit that "murder is murder." Your compromises and justifications are woefully inadequate. 28 Abortion is a repugnant and reprehensible evil in the sight of God. Is there wailing among the redeemed over this outrage or does the Church no longer fear God? Why do you tolerate men coercing women to kill their sons and daughters? 29 Do not be deceived. God will avenge the bloodshed of His precious ones.

30 Meanwhile, many of you will claim to be concerned about the unborn, but very few have taken steps to put action to your words. Some of you speak passionately about this injustice as you ought, but do nothing to tangibly care for the lives of babies and destitute mothers. 31 Collectively, we have the means to eliminate the need for women to terminate their pregnancies. We are capable of providing them with medical care and giving their unwanted children a loving home. 32 How can the nation

WHORING BRIDE

be expected to believe what we say regarding the sanctity of life when so few of us are willing to be inconvenienced for their sake? 33 By now, we should have cleared out all the orphanages because of our willingness to look after those with no parents. There should be no children bouncing around the foster care system because Christians ought to have been first in line to care for the neglected. 34 The world will start believing that we love mankind as Christ does when we begin sacrificing our abundance to help those in desperate circumstances.

35 Some of you will claim that the liberties afforded to us in our founding documents are a divine blessing. And so they are! 36 It is true what the Psalmist said, *"Blessed is the nation whose God is the LORD."* 37 But make no mistake brothers and sisters, even if we could agree that America is the greatest nation ever to exist, it is still a kingdom of this world. 38 Suppose we agreed that America was founded on Christian principles and that our nation would better flourish if we fashioned our laws in the likeness of God's law. 39 We know perfectly well from history that we cannot create faith with legislation. Obedience to God is a matter of the heart—one that is yielded to Him only by the effective grace of the gospel. 40 We will do more to "Christianize" America through our compelling witness than any vote we cast or laws we pass. Laboring to preserve the freedoms we inherited is not wrong, but doing so must not come at the expense of abandoning our high calling to live as salt and light in the world. 41 Too many of us have entered into the fray of political discourse, employing worldly tactics to achieve partisan victories.

42 I want to remind you, brothers and sisters, that our battle is not against politicians or party platforms. Our foe is the ancient Serpent and his demonic minions. 43 Your embarrassment of this reality does not nullify their existence. 44 These evil forces were given limited authority on Earth until God consigns them to eternal punishment. Their agenda is chaos, misery, and destruction for all of mankind. Sowing hateful discord is their trademark. 45 Be mindful of your true enemy and recall what the Apostle Paul wrote to the church in Ephesus: *"For we do not wrestle against flesh and blood, but against the rulers, against the authorities, against the cosmic powers over this present darkness, against the spiritual forces of evil in the heavenly places."*

46 Though we may never fully agree on policy ideas, our political engagement ought to be controlled by love for one another. 47 We should be an example to the watching world of how to peaceably disagree while still working together for the greater good. Instead of arguing and fighting as the world does, we should band together in unity as we seek the welfare and prosperity of our nation. 48 Rather than dividing ourselves into the political options offered to us, we should act as the moral conscience of our elected leaders. 49 Political consternation is not an excuse for civic disengagement. You are free to vote and advocate for certain policies, but in doing so, take steps to avoid being sucked into endless arguments.

50 There are no generic candidates or platforms, so we will inevitably have to deal with political parties. Therefore, make it your aim not to be held hostage by certain affiliations. 51 We are in a unique position to have a prophetic voice as children

of light in a dark world, for we know what is the ultimate hope for mankind. 52 Our churches were designated to be the metaphorical hands and feet of Jesus to the nations. 53 To truly love our neighbors, we must be politically active. Do not forget our primary mandate to love God with all heart, soul, mind, and strength, and to love others (including our enemies) with the same fervor and attention that we afford ourselves. 54 God expects His Church in America to be politically prophetic, not partisan.

55 Here we have an opportunity to regain some lost credibility as we engage in the politics of our day. We ought to be more active than all other citizens as we work together to meet the needs of our communities. 56 Politicians should feel obliged to accommodate our ethical demands rather than manipulate us as pawns in their quests for power.

57 Our nation seems irreconcilably divided, and vitriol is spewed from both sides. Do not be discouraged by this. 58 God is greater than any nation and the love of Christ can transform enemies into friends. Jesus stated that He has already overcome the world. 59 His kingdom will come, eventually righting all the wrongs in America. Our conduct in the present age ought to be a preview for the divine restoration that is to come. 60 Let us, therefore, drop any notion of political enemies. In the kingdom of God, we love our enemies. We serve and pray for those who oppose us. 61 If the Church remains compromised by political divisions, there is no hope for America. But if we can rise above divisiveness, demonstrating self-sacrificing love for our neighbors despite our differences, then the Church can be the healing balm our country needs.

Chapter 6: Repentance

1 When someone unlawfully ventures into a space or remains in that space when asked to leave, such a one is considered a trespasser. We understand this concept regarding earthly property laws but seem to have forgotten that Scripture describes sin as the trespassing of God's law. 2 The boundaries of human behavior established by God are not optional. They are to be honored, not ignored. 3 Scripture further explains that everyone is guilty of trespassing God's law. All are sinners; none are blameless. 4 We manufacture all sorts of justifications to excuse our sinful behavior, but who are you, O trespasser, to question the boundaries laid down by your Maker?

5 I want to remind you, brothers and sisters, that until our lowly bodies are made perfect on the last day, the Christian life will require continual repentance. 6 We were redeemed from eternal destruction and adopted back into the family of God when we first believed in Christ. But upon believing we were not instantly changed into what we will become when our salvation is completed.

7 In our present state, we are undergoing the slow process of sanctification. Until death, all of us will daily wrestle with the temptation to sin. 8 Though we belong to Christ, the fallen desire to return to our former ways of living is inevitable. 9 Our gullible and fickle hearts will regularly be lured away by the idols of our culture. Our bodies will be seduced by the lustful cravings of sexual sin. 10 We will constantly be charmed by the power and comforts of wealth. The desire to self-justify and rule others will draw us toward acquiring political power. 11 There are a host of sins that threaten to distract us, thwarting our faithful obedience

to Christ. Even our eagerness to serve God can be perverted into damnable self-righteousness.

12 In this life one thing is clear: we are utterly dependent upon God's grace to walk in obedience. When we fall into the clutches of sin, without delay we must confess those sins. Thanks be to God that forgiveness is readily available to all who would genuinely seek it. 13 But we should not stop there. Along with forgiveness, we should ask God for the empowering grace of the Spirit to transform us into ever-increasing degrees of holiness.

14 Do not fashion your morality by the values of American culture, for they are contrary to those in the kingdom of God. Let Scripture be your guide. 15 Thus did Paul write in his letter to Timothy: "*All Scripture is breathed out by God and profitable for teaching, for reproof, for correction, and for training in righteousness, that the man of God may be complete, equipped for every good work.*" 16 Make no mistake, we do not need to rescue the Bible from cultural embarrassment. It is we who need to be rescued from this wicked and adulterous generation by the liberating truth of Scripture at work within us. 17 Rightly did the Psalmist say, "*The sum of your word is truth, and every one of your righteous rules endures forever.*" 18 Recounting the story of God providing manna in the wilderness, our Lord Jesus reinforced this idea when He was tempted in the desert saying, "*It is written, 'Man shall not live by bread alone, but by every word that comes from the mouth of God.'*" 19 And in His high priestly prayer for all believers, Jesus asked the Father, "*Sanctify them in the truth; your word is truth.*"

20 Though we are not bound by the law of Moses—for none are justified by works of the law—we are obligated to obey what

the Apostle Paul called "*the law of Christ.*" 21 To a degree, the law of Christ calls us to a higher standard than even the law of Moses because it targets the heart, not merely external actions. 22 Jesus said, "*You have heard that it was said, 'You shall not commit adultery.' But I say to you that everyone who looks at a woman with lustful intent has already committed adultery with her in his heart,*" 23 and "*You have heard that it was said to those of old, 'You shall not murder; and whoever murders will be liable to judgment.' But I say to you that everyone who is angry with his brother will be liable to judgment; whoever insults his brother will be liable to the council; and whoever says, 'You fool!' will be liable to the hell of fire.*" 24 Additionally, He taught, "*You have heard that it was said, 'You shall love your neighbor and hate your enemy.' But I say to you, Love your enemies and pray for those who persecute you, so that you may be sons of your Father who is in heaven.*" 25 Our being made righteous through Christ does not negate His expectation for obedience. 26 Elsewhere Jesus said, "*Why do you call me 'Lord, Lord,' and not do what I tell you?*" 27 This still applies to believers today. How can we call ourselves followers of Christ if we insist on rejecting His commands, choosing instead to follow the dictates of our culture? 28 He is not our Lord if we view obedience to His commands as optional.

29 When Jesus went public with His ministry as God's Messiah, He traveled from town to town telling crowds, "*Repent, for the kingdom of heaven is at hand.*" 30 Our ignorance in understanding this part of the Master's teaching has led to much confusion. Many of us wrongly assume He was commanding the crowds to grovel on their hands and knees, lamenting their sinful behavior. 31 Though confession of sin is essential to salvation,

this is not what Jesus was communicating. 32 When the Lord called for people to *"repent,"* He used a word that denotes a reorientation of one's mind. It was an invitation to fundamentally transform our outlook on God's involvement in the world.

33 The central purpose of the Father's redemptive plan was to inaugurate God's kingdom rule on Earth just as it is in Heaven. This included saving sinners from their deserved condemnation for the praise of His glory and grace. 34 And much like a seed that is buried can grow up to overtake an entire garden, so is the kingdom of God gradually taking over the world through the loving deeds of people redeemed by the gospel.

35 So if the gospel is going to eventually capture the entire world, one might ask, "Why then does evil persist?" 36 Jesus told a parable to illustrate how evil will grow and spread along with the gospel until the last day. 37 He said, *"The kingdom of heaven may be compared to a man who sowed good seed in his field, but while his men were sleeping, his enemy came and sowed weeds among the wheat and went away. So when the plants came up and bore grain, then the weeds appeared also. And the servants of the master of the house came and said to him, 'Master, did you not sow good seed in your field? How then does it have weeds?' He said to them, 'An enemy has done this.' So the servants said to him, 'Then do you want us to go and gather them?' But he said, 'No, lest in gathering the weeds you root up the wheat along with them. Let both grow together until the harvest, and at harvest time I will tell the reapers, 'Gather the weeds first and bind them in bundles to be burned, but gather the wheat into my barn.'"*

38 The evil in our world is represented by the weeds in this parable. It will continue to grow alongside the gradual but full

acceptance of the gospel within every nation. 39 In the end, the Master will sort out the bad from the good on the day of His great harvest. If we are to learn anything from this illustration, it is that evil will continue to expand and flourish until the Lord returns. Knowing this, we are to guard ourselves from the wiles of temptation. 40 Jude, the earthly brother of Jesus, wrote in his epistle, "'*In the last time there will be scoffers, following their own ungodly passions.' It is these who cause divisions, worldly people, devoid of the Spirit. But you, beloved, building yourselves up in your most holy faith and praying in the Holy Spirit, keep yourselves in the love of God, waiting for the mercy of our Lord Jesus Christ that leads to eternal life. And have mercy on those who doubt; save others by snatching them out of the fire; to others show mercy with fear, hating even the garment stained by the flesh.*"

41 These instructions are clear. We are to separate ourselves from the ungodly deeds of this world, hating the very taint of sin. 42 This doesn't mean that we are prohibited from dealing with unbelievers, for that would contradict what Scripture teaches elsewhere about loving our neighbors and seeking the *shalom* of our communities. 43 Rather, we are to draw distinct boundaries as outlined in Scripture around what we will and will not participate in. We are commanded to love the people of this world in the manner of Christ Jesus but are forbidden from joining them in their misdeeds.

44 To be faithful witnesses of the gospel we must resolutely and militantly combat the temptation to sin. Knowing our propensity for choosing evil, we must commit ourselves to holy living as we wait for Christ's return to make all things new. 45 Whenever we fail in this regard, we should confess our sins, and seek His strengthening grace to walk in obedience.

WHORING BRIDE

46 Confessing sin as individuals is vital, but we ought also to consider regular corporate confession within our gatherings. 47 Scripture is replete with examples of the people of God coming together to corporately pray and fast, seeking God's mercy for the sins of the larger society. 48 As ambassadors of Heaven, we are like watchmen at the gate who have fallen asleep. Our country is guilty of many grievous sins—some with the open participation and endorsement of our churches. 49 Let us, therefore, confess our sins individually and corporately so that we may be found blameless and without stain at His return.

50 Regarding your worship gatherings, I'm grieved by how little time and energy is being devoted to prayer. Have you forgotten what aroused the anger of our Lord? 51 When Jesus saw the temple leaders of His day neglecting prayerful devotion but busying themselves with commerce and religious transactions, angry zeal for His Father's house consumed Him. 52 Matthew records the incident saying, *"And Jesus entered the temple and drove out all who sold and bought in the temple, and he overturned the tables of the money-changers and the seats of those who sold pigeons. He said to them, 'It is written, 'My house shall be called a house of prayer,' but you make it a den of robbers.'"*

53 Much of your religious activity is empty and powerless because you are not abiding in Christ and have neglected to seek God in fervent prayer. 54 The Almighty is an infinite reservoir of wisdom and power. So why are we content with stillborn worship resulting from prayerlessness when a banqueting table of His fullness is available to us? 55 Sermons have their place; as does music, giving, and the administration of the sacraments.

But prayer ought not to be an afterthought. It should define and control all ministries within your congregations.

56 Brothers and sisters, communion with the great I AM awaits you in the prayer closet. There is no shortcut or substitute for regularly encountering God besides the accumulated hours of earnest prayer. And let the overflow of private devotion shape your corporate gatherings such that they can once again be called *"a house of prayer."*

Chapter 7: Unity

1 Brothers and sisters, I have written sternly about our many flaws, but not without hope. 2 My confidence in the ultimate victory of the universal Church is unwavering because Christ is a mighty savior! 3 In Scripture, we are promised that God will surely accomplish His plans in the world. 4 Sin and death were struck a fatal blow with the empty tomb and will be utterly conquered in the end. Christ's eternal reign will be permanently established on Earth, and all His enemies will be made a footstool. 5 The outcome is not in doubt. What remains to be seen is whether or not the churches in America will join in His triumph.

6 Proximity to the message of the gospel is not the same thing as participation in the kingdom of God. Simply attending worship services and making faith claims that have little or no impact on our lives is no guarantee that we belong to Christ.

7 Jesus said, "*Not everyone who says to me, 'Lord, Lord,' will enter the kingdom of heaven, but the one who does the will of my Father who is in heaven. On that day many will say to me, 'Lord, Lord, did we not prophesy in your name, and cast out demons in your name, and do many mighty works in your name?' And then will I declare to them, 'I never knew you; depart from me, you workers of lawlessness.'*" 8 It is not enough to merely pay lip service by calling Him "Lord." Note that Jesus indicated on the last day, it will not be a meager few, but **many** who will be turned away. Though they call him "Lord" they will be rejected because they did not do the will of His Father, regardless of what theatrics they did in His name.

9 In other parts of the world, following Jesus comes with a high price. Many of our brothers and sisters around the globe end up losing careers and relationships when they surrender their lives to Christ. 10 They are subjected to persecution and humiliation. Some are imprisoned and even put to death. 11 Costly discipleship is a foreign concept to us because we have overly domesticated the gospel. We've castrated the message of the kingdom so that we bear virtually no cost whatsoever. 12 We have ignored the words of Jesus: *"If anyone would come after me, let him deny himself and take up his cross and follow me. For whoever would save his life will lose it, but whoever loses his life for my sake and the gospel's will save it. For what does it profit a man to gain the whole world and forfeit his soul? For what can a man give in return for his soul? For whoever is ashamed of me and of my words in this adulterous and sinful generation, of him will the Son of Man also be ashamed when he comes in the glory of his Father with the holy angels."*

13 The Christian life is one of perpetual self-denial. 14 That is not to say it is a life without joy and rewards. There are incomparable delights that accompany living in harmony with our Maker. 15 We receive foretastes of our joy's ultimate consummation as we follow Jesus, but life on Earth in comparison to eternity is but a momentary vapor. 16 Therefore we should gladly embrace whatever temporary sacrifices are necessary in obedience to Christ, knowing that whatever pleasures or comforts we give up in this life will be repaid to us a thousandfold in the age to come.

17 This is why Jesus instructed us in His famous sermon, *"Do not lay up for yourselves treasures on earth, where moth and*

rust destroy and where thieves break in and steal, but lay up for yourselves treasures in heaven, where neither moth nor rust destroys and where thieves do not break in and steal. For where your treasure is, there your heart will be also." 18 If our ultimate reward is earthly treasures, the affection of our hearts will reside with the corruptible and fleeting pleasures of this world. But if we are willing to delay full gratification in this world and locate our treasure in Heaven, immeasurable rewards will be ours forevermore.

19 Does this describe American Christianity? If we are not willing to lay down our personal pursuits and grab a cross, we must ask ourselves whether or not we truly belong to Him.

20 Faithfully following Jesus in America sounds impossible, but hallelujah, with God all things are possible. 21 Saint Peter wrote in his epistle, *"His divine power has granted to us all things that pertain to life and godliness, through the knowledge of him who called us to his own glory and excellence, by which he has granted to us his precious and very great promises, so that through them you may become partakers of the divine nature, having escaped from the corruption that is in the world because of sinful desire. For this very reason, make every effort to supplement your faith with virtue, and virtue with knowledge, and knowledge with self-control, and self-control with steadfastness, and steadfastness with godliness, and godliness with brotherly affection, and brotherly affection with love. For if these qualities are yours and are increasing, they keep you from being ineffective or unfruitful in the knowledge of our Lord Jesus Christ."*

22 Therefore brothers and sisters, let us consecrate ourselves to Christ so that we may faithfully bear witness to the truth of the gospel. This begins with our commitment to not just love our

neighbors but to each other also. 23 Recall the words of our Lord who said, "*A new commandment I give to you, that you love one another: just as I have loved you, you also are to love one another. By this all people will know that you are my disciples, if you have love for one another.*" 24 Scripture is clear that the distinguishing mark of our discipleship to an observing world is in the manner with which we love each other.

25 We come from different traditions, but let us not forget that there is only one Lord, one gospel, and one bride of Christ. 26 We congregate around varying points of theological emphasis. Some focus on the gifts of the Spirit. Some focus on expositional preaching. Others prioritize liturgical formulations. Some even define themselves by the absence of denominational affiliation. 27 We do not share total agreement on practices of the eucharist or baptism, nor do we all agree on matters of scriptural interpretation, liturgy, and hierarchical leadership structures.

28 Whereas these differences understandably cause us to gravitate toward certain expressions of worship over others, we must not lose sight of the fact that we serve the same Master. 29 The universal church is described in Scripture as the "*body of Christ.*" Some are like a hand, others like a foot or an eye, but we are all connected as different parts of the same body with Christ Jesus as our head.

30 As we wrestle to understand the full counsel of God, the disunity between our various traditions surely grieves the Father's heart. 31 The human body experiences disease when its parts are not functioning together in harmony as they ought. So it is with the body of Christ. We experience depleted spiritual health by our unwillingness to cooperate on a unified front. 32

Simply because your brother or sister across town has a different nuanced opinion than you on secondary theological matters does not nullify our obligation to love them and view them as family members in the faith. 33 Our shared mission suffers when we allow our differences to prevent cooperation.

34 Divisions of race, gender, class, education, and political philosophies are currently fracturing our society. Rather than offering our culture a model of peaceful coexistence despite our differences, we are allowing that same divisive spirit to rupture the unity among believers that God desires.

35 Consider the words that John wrote in his epistle to the disunified believers in his day: *"Beloved, let us love one another, for love is from God, and whoever loves has been born of God and knows God. Anyone who does not love does not know God, because God is love. In this the love of God was made manifest among us, that God sent his only Son into the world, so that we might live through him. In this is love, not that we have loved God but that he loved us and sent his Son to be the propitiation for our sins. Beloved, if God so loved us, we also ought to love one another. No one has ever seen God; if we love one another, God abides in us and his love is perfected in us."* 36 Our mandate is to love our neighbors and to love our enemies, but even more important than this is the love that we show towards one another, for this is how the world will know that we are the redeemed people of God.

37 Disunity among the churches in America is a cancer within the body of Christ. The success or failure of our legacy hangs on our ability to love each other despite our differences. 38 Here the temptation to self-justify is strong, for we all secretly wish to believe God favors our particular sect because of our

theological correctness. 39 But what good is our theology if we do not have love? 40 On this point, the words of Paul to the Corinthian church are instructive: *"If I speak in the tongues of men and of angels, but have not love, I am a noisy gong or a clanging cymbal. And if I have prophetic powers, and understand all mysteries and all knowledge, and if I have all faith, so as to remove mountains, but have not love, I am nothing. If I give away all I have, and if I deliver up my body to be burned, but have not love, I gain nothing."*

41 For the sake of the gospel flourishing in our great land, let us consider how we can build unity between our church traditions. 42 There are many joint ventures in serving our communities that we can participate in together without having to surrender our theological distinctives. 43 To our shame, we may not be ready to gather around a common Lord's table (though that would be a marvelous achievement), but maybe we could start building unity by sharing meals together. 44 Pastors fellowshipping with other pastors of different denominations would be a positive example for their parishioners. 45 Believers young and old, of different races and from different backgrounds breaking bread together will go a long way in repairing our disunified fellowships. 46 However difficult it may be to cultivate friendships across traditions and denominations, remember this: God desires for us to be unified while Satan desires for us to remain divided.

47 Tearing down the walls of division within the body of Christ in America will only happen when we begin viewing each other as part of a singular spiritual family. Then perhaps America will know that we are true disciples of Jesus. 48 Let us then

prioritize marching together under the common banner of the kingdom of God, and may our love for each other overpower all forces threatening to divide us.

Chapter 8: Conclusion

1 The skeptics of His day approached Jesus and asked for a supernatural sign to validate the claims He was making. Jesus rebuked them for not being able to discern the signs of their time. 2 He said, *"When it is evening, you say, 'It will be fair weather, for the sky is red.' And in the morning, 'It will be stormy today, for the sky is red and threatening.' You know how to interpret the appearance of the sky, but you cannot interpret the signs of the times. An evil and adulterous generation seeks for a sign, but no sign will be given to it except the sign of Jonah."* 3 If skeptics and detractors then were expected to evaluate their cultural moment, how much more should the redeemed sons and daughters of God who have the Holy Spirit be able to understand the days in which they are living?

4 The "sign of Jonah" was in essence a warning of forthcoming destruction if they failed to repent. 5 Brothers and sisters, can we not see the storm clouds gathering overhead? A clear-sighted survey of our land shows that the hour is late and the days are ripe with wickedness. 6 The Apostle Paul wrote in his letter to young Timothy, *"But understand this, that in the last days there will come times of difficulty. For people will be lovers of self, lovers of money, proud, arrogant, abusive, disobedient to their parents, ungrateful, unholy, heartless, unappeasable, slanderous, without self-control, brutal, not loving good, treacherous, reckless, swollen with conceit, lovers of pleasure rather than lovers of God, having the appearance of godliness, but denying its power."* 7 Does this not perfectly describe the days in which we are living? We may think it unlikely that we are the inhabitants of the world in

its final stage, but eventually, that day will arrive and the Church must be ready.

8 No man knows the exact day or hour of Christ's return. We cannot know for sure if we are living in the "last days," but we do know that we are closer to that terrible and blessed moment than any generation before us. 9 When His followers asked about the last days, Jesus said, "*See that no one leads you astray. For many will come in my name, saying, 'I am the Christ,' and they will lead many astray. And you will hear of wars and rumors of wars. See that you are not alarmed, for this must take place, but the end is not yet. For nation will rise against nation, and kingdom against kingdom, and there will be famines and earthquakes in various places. All these are but the beginning of the birth pains. Then they will deliver you up to tribulation and put you to death, and you will be hated by all nations for my name's sake. And then many will fall away and betray one another and hate one another. And many false prophets will arise and lead many astray. And because lawlessness will be increased, the love of many will grow cold. But the one who endures to the end will be saved. And this gospel of the kingdom will be proclaimed throughout the whole world as a testimony to all nations, and then the end will come.*" 10 These words no doubt had a specific application to His original hearers. So is this teaching meaningless to us in our day, or might they also contain a larger warning of things to come?

11 Scripture predicts in the last days there will be a rebellion against the truth of the gospel and that a great apostasy will unfold whereby many professing believers are deceived and fall away from the faith. 12 Whether those days are upon us now or still a ways off, the question of faithfulness remains before us. 13 We Americans come from a rich heritage of pioneering

self-reliance and a perceived sense of invincibility, but do not be deceived dear ones. 14 Remember the words of James who said, *"You adulterous people! Do you not know that friendship with the world is enmity with God? Therefore whoever wishes to be a friend of the world makes himself an enemy of God. Or do you suppose it is to no purpose that the Scripture says, 'He yearns jealously over the spirit that he has made to dwell in us'? But he gives more grace. Therefore it says, 'God opposes the proud but gives grace to the humble.'"*

15 Brothers and sisters, where is your trembling? Flirting with temptation and seeking friendship with wickedness is like assuming a posture of military opposition against the Almighty. 16 Have we so profaned the sacred that we are no longer staggered in awe by His glory and majesty? Is it out of ignorance or defiance that we ignore what the author of Hebrews said in his epistle? 17 *"For if we go on sinning deliberately after receiving the knowledge of the truth, there no longer remains a sacrifice for sins, but a fearful expectation of judgment, and a fury of fire that will consume the adversaries. Anyone who has set aside the law of Moses dies without mercy on the evidence of two or three witnesses. How much worse punishment, do you think, will be deserved by the one who has trampled underfoot the Son of God, and has profaned the blood of the covenant by which he was sanctified, and has outraged the Spirit of grace? For we know him who said, 'Vengeance is mine; I will repay.' And again, 'The Lord will judge his people.' It is a fearful thing to fall into the hands of the living God."*

18 To the pastors and leaders within our churches, I implore you to consider these words and shepherd the flock of God as ones who will give an account. Their spiritual maturity is under your care. 19 You have been warned in Scripture that those of

you presuming to be teachers will be held to a higher standard since believers are charged to follow your instruction. 20 Heed the words of God through the prophet Isaiah when Israel mixed their worship with idolatry: *"What to me is the multitude of your sacrifices? says the LORD; I have had enough of burnt offerings of rams and the fat of well-fed beasts; I do not delight in the blood of bulls, or of lambs, or of goats. When you come to appear before me, who has required of you this trampling of my courts? Bring no more vain offerings; incense is an abomination to me. New moon and Sabbath and the calling of convocations—I cannot endure iniquity and solemn assembly. Your new moons and your appointed feasts my soul hates; they have become a burden to me; I am weary of bearing them. When you spread out your hands, I will hide my eyes from you; even though you make many prayers, I will not listen; your hands are full of blood."* 21 And likewise, the words of God through the prophet Amos: *"I hate, I despise your feasts, and I take no delight in your solemn assemblies. Even though you offer me your burnt offerings and grain offerings, I will not accept them; and the peace offerings of your fattened animals, I will not look upon them. Take away from me the noise of your songs; to the melody of your harps I will not listen. But let justice roll down like waters, and righteousness like an ever-flowing stream."* 22 If this was God's reaction to the corrupted worship services of His people under the old covenant which was inferior and fading away, how much more zealous is He for the pure, unadulterated worship of partakers in the new covenant? 23 Your worship services may garner the applause of man, but if you do not address the idolatry within your gatherings are you so foolish to think God will be pleased by your religious exercises? 24 Our

God is a consuming fire, jealous for the pure worship of His people. He is the same yesterday, today, and forever.

25 To those who are not in leadership positions but count yourselves a part of the American Church, I appeal to your love of Jesus Christ. Separate yourselves from the filth of our culture and live holy lives of devotion to the One who redeemed you from sin. 26 You are bombarded with alluring temptations, but God has placed the Holy Spirit within you as a helper so that you may no longer walk according to the patterns of this world. 27 Meditate on the words of Saint Paul in his letter to Titus: *"For we ourselves were once foolish, disobedient, led astray, slaves to various passions and pleasures, passing our days in malice and envy, hated by others and hating one another. But when the goodness and loving kindness of God our Savior appeared, he saved us, not because of works done by us in righteousness, but according to his own mercy, by the washing of regeneration and renewal of the Holy Spirit, whom he poured out on us richly through Jesus Christ our Savior, so that being justified by his grace we might become heirs according to the hope of eternal life."* 28 Whatever the cost, pursue the approval of God over the approval of your culture. Throw down the idols of your heart, smashing them to bits. 29 Pledge your undying loyalty to Christ so that you may be numbered among the faithful remnant God is preserving for Himself in our land.

30 Consider again the parable of the sower. Jesus said, *"A sower went out to sow. And as he sowed, some seeds fell along the path, and the birds came and devoured them. Other seeds fell on rocky ground, where they did not have much soil, and immediately they sprang up, since they had no depth of soil, but when the sun rose they were scorched. And since they had no root, they withered*

away. Other seeds fell among thorns, and the thorns grew up and choked them. Other seeds fell on good soil and produced grain, some a hundredfold, some sixty, some thirty. He who has ears, let him hear." 31 Confused by this parable His disciples asked for an explanation. Jesus answered, *"Hear then the parable of the sower: When anyone hears the word of the kingdom and does not understand it, the evil one comes and snatches away what has been sown in his heart. This is what was sown along the path. As for what was sown on rocky ground, this is the one who hears the word and immediately receives it with joy, yet he has no root in himself, but endures for a while, and when tribulation or persecution arises on account of the word, immediately he falls away. As for what was sown among thorns, this is the one who hears the word, but the cares of the world and the deceitfulness of riches choke the word, and it proves unfruitful. As for what was sown on good soil, this is the one who hears the word and understands it. He indeed bears fruit and yields, in one case a hundredfold, in another sixty, and in another thirty."*

32 The question lingers: when the seed of Christ's words came to you, what kind of soil was there to receive it? 33 Did you hasten with emotion to welcome it, but as the blazing sun of opposition from our culture beat down on you, it scorched what was sown in you? Might it be then, that the soil of your heart was shallow and rocky, making it impossible to bear any fruit? 34 Or did you receive the word, but the cares of this world like sensual pleasures and the desire for riches choke out any potential growth? 35 Better still, did you receive the word of Christ by allowing it to take root in your heart no matter what hardships you encountered? Is that which was sown in you bearing fruit? 36 These are difficult teachings. I pray to the Lord

of the harvest He tills the soil of our hearts, cultivating us into bearing much fruit.

37 We inherited a country bestowed with greatness, but she is guilty of many sins. God will settle accounts with her in due time. 38 Therefore, let us seek mercy and grace while it is available. 39 May the word of the Lord to Solomon be true of America as well when He said, "*if my people who are called by my name humble themselves, and pray and seek my face and turn from their wicked ways, then I will hear from heaven and will forgive their sin and heal their land.*"

40 Though my words to you have been harsh, please know that it is only because my love for you runs deep. 41 A notable proverb from King Solomon says, "*Faithful are the wounds of a friend; profuse are the kisses of an enemy.*" 42 I love my country and I love the bride of Christ. I long to see America redeemed and sanctified, not destroyed by divine judgment. 43 O God, have mercy on us. Forgive our sins and give us the strength to walk in faithful obedience no matter the cost. 44 May the words of Christ be true of us, when America observes the compelling beauty of our lives: "*In the same way, let your light shine before others, so that they may see your good works and give glory to your Father who is in heaven.*"

45 I leave you with Jude's doxology: "*Now to him who is able to keep you from stumbling and to present you blameless before the presence of his glory with great joy, to the only God, our Savior, through Jesus Christ our Lord, be glory, majesty, dominion, and authority, before all time and now and forever. Amen.*"

Afterword (for the younger generations)

In a letter to his young protege Timothy, the Apostle Paul wrote, "*Command and teach these things. Let no one despise you for your youth, but set the believers an example in speech, in conduct, in love, in faith, in purity.*"

To students in middle school, high school, and college along with the young professionals in our churches, I want to issue a challenge: do better than those who came before you. The preceding generations have largely failed you. It was their job to pass on to you the torch of faith which they received. What you stand to inherit from them is a far cry from the Church as Jesus or the early apostles imagined it.

There are many churches in America, very few of which are experiencing the regular presence and power of God in their midst. The chapters of this book address several of the contributing factors as to why God is noticeably absent in our gatherings. I urge you to learn from their poor example and resolve to forge a different legacy.

In the Old Testament when Asa ruled over Judah, Hanani the seer was sent to rebuke him for cutting deals with other nations rather than trusting in God. He told the king, "*For the eyes of the Lord run to and fro throughout the whole earth, to give strong support to those whose heart is blameless toward him. You have done foolishly in this, for from now on you will have wars.*" God had delivered improbable victories to His people in the past and Asa knew as much. And yet, rather than looking once again to receive Heaven's help, the king relied on his own judgment.

Because of this foolish mistake, they lost their divine protection and wars ensued.

I bring this story up because it teaches us something valuable about our Maker. We read that God's eyes are fixed on earth, roaming back and forth in search of hearts that are wholly blameless toward Him. He stands ready to give strong support to such hearts wherever He finds them. You can distinguish yourselves as a generation steadfastly devoted to God, despite the failures of our present-day Church. In the face of immense temptation and cultural pressure, you have the opportunity to part from the example of your spiritual parents and manifest the power and presence of God by becoming the Church in America as it was intended to be.

I pray our churches awake from their stupor, recognize the prevailing unfaithfulness, and humbly return to the Lord in repentance. But if they persist in recalcitrance and spiritual infidelity, for the sake of His great name and to the praise of His glory I pray that your generation will heap burning coals on their heads by taking up the mantle of true discipleship which they have neglected. Plant a flag in the ground and refuse to cede any territory to the Enemy. Push back in the power of the Holy Spirit and ask God to break the backbone of the dark forces in our land. Stand fearlessly in opposition to the corrupting influences of our world and watch the victory of God unfold before your very eyes.

He stands ready to help us as He did the Psalmist who wrote, "*I waited patiently for the Lord; he inclined to me and heard my cry. He drew me up from the pit of destruction, out of the miry bog, and set my feet upon a rock, making my steps secure. He put a new song in my mouth, a song of praise to our God. Many will see and fear, and put their trust in the Lord. Blessed is the man who makes the Lord his trust, who does not turn to the proud, to those who go astray after a lie! You have multiplied, O Lord my God, your wondrous deeds and your thoughts toward us; none can compare with you! I will proclaim and tell of them, yet they are more than can be told. In sacrifice and offering you have not delighted, but you have given me an open ear. Burnt offering and sin offering you have not required. Then I said, 'Behold, I have come; in the scroll of the book it is written of me: I delight to do your will, O my God; your law is within my heart.' I have told the glad news of deliverance in the great congregation; behold, I have not restrained my lips, as you know, O Lord. I have not hidden your deliverance within my heart; I have spoken of your faithfulness and your salvation; I have not concealed your steadfast love and your faithfulness from the great congregation. As for you, O Lord, you will not restrain your mercy from me; your steadfast love and your faithfulness will ever preserve me! For evils have encompassed me beyond number; my iniquities have overtaken me, and I cannot see; they are more than the hairs of my head; my heart fails me. Be pleased, O Lord, to deliver me! O Lord, make haste to help me! Let those be put to shame and disappointed altogether who seek to snatch away my life; let those be turned back and brought to dishonor who delight in my hurt! Let those be appalled because of their shame who say to me, 'Aha, Aha!' But may all who seek you rejoice and be glad in you; may those who love your salvation say continually, 'Great is the Lord!' As for me, I am poor and needy, but the Lord takes thought for me. You are my help and my deliverer; do not delay, O my God!"*

Whereas your predecessors have played the whore and gone after worldliness, and though you face seemingly insurmountable evil, mercy is available nonetheless. Forgiveness is one prayer away. God's love is immeasurable. His wisdom is unsearchable. His grace is unfathomable. His mercy is incomprehensible, and His power is endless.

The Prophet Habakkuk prayed, *"O Lord, I have heard the report of you, and your work, O Lord, do I fear. In the midst of the years revive it; in the midst of the years make it known; in wrath remember mercy."* Such is the prayer of this author for the churches in America. We know the mighty deeds of God throughout history. O, that He would renew them again in our day! Revivals and awakenings have swept through our country in the past. Even now there are stirrings of spiritual hunger on campuses. A growing distaste for the poisons of this world is spreading. God has preserved a faithful remnant in our land. May we join their ranks and pull Heaven's glory downward through prayer and unyielding devotion.

Jesus told His disciples *"Truly, truly, I say to you, whoever believes in me will also do the works that I do; and greater works than these will he do, because I am going to the Father. Whatever you ask in my name, this I will do, that the Father may be glorified in the Son. If you ask me anything in my name, I will do it. If you love me, you will keep my commandments. And I will ask the Father, and he will give you another Helper, to be with you forever, even the Spirit of truth, whom the world cannot receive, because it neither sees him nor knows him. You know him, for he dwells with you and will be in you."* This is a staggering teaching. It cannot apply only to the first apostles because Jesus directed it toward *"whoever believes in me."* And the strength of the promise is conditional upon the presence of the indwelling Holy Spirit, which is given to all believers. It seems as if Jesus were daring us to go beyond even what He did while on earth.

WHORING BRIDE

Can you see the potential for churches in America today? Why do we forfeit such wonderful promises for the fleeting pleasures of sin? A stalwart presence of faithful Christianity in America would not only honor God but quite literally change the world. And remember, we do not conquer like the kingdoms of this world. We advance the kingdom of God every time we proclaim the truth of the gospel, turn the other cheek, walk a second mile, feed the hungry, and clothe the naked. We defeat the darkness when we give generously and sacrificially. The triumph of Jesus becomes tangible when we love our enemies and pray for those who mistreat us. If we can keep our lives uncontaminated by the world as we follow Christ in faithful obedience, we will witness His kingdom come and His will done here in America, just as it is in Heaven.

Those with ears to hear, let them hear. May the bride of Christ in America arise and return to her Bridegroom. To God alone be the glory, both now and forever.

Don't miss out!

Visit the website below and you can sign up to receive emails whenever Elijah Washington publishes a new book. There's no charge and no obligation.

https://books2read.com/r/B-A-KRVY-GRCKC

Connecting independent readers to independent writers.

* 9 7 9 8 2 2 3 6 4 6 0 2 0 *